To Denise and Carlitos:

"Always Believe!"

LICENSE NOTES:

This book remains the copyrighted property of the author, and may not be redistributed to others for commercial or non-commercial purposes.

Thank you for your support.

Published and Illustrated by Marlene Kaltschmitt

Copyright 2014 Marlene Kaltschmitt

Printed in The United States of America

ISBN-13:978-1499294712

ISBN-10:1499294719

Suzy Lu and The Mustard Seed

By Marlene Kaltschmitt

This BOOK was inspired by Mathew 17:20

Jesus told His disciples,
"Because of your little faith.
For truly, I say to you,
if you have
faith like a grain of
MUSTARD SEED
you will say to this mountain, '
Move from here to there,' and it will
move, and nothing
will be impossible for you."

Today Suzy Lu received many gifts,
What a SURPRISE!
But of all the birthday gifts she got,
the smallest one caught her eye.

A small gift with a big bow,
she wonders, "What could it be?"
Something small, it appears...

She unties the bow, and here is what she sees:
A little box inside of the small one?!

This was gifted with care.
Suzy Lu was excited.
Her eyes were glowing with cheer.

Wow, it is a gold chain necklace, with a crystal ball hanging beneath.

It has a mustard seed inside.
It´s quite a **MASTERPIECE!**

She holds it up in the air,
and then draws it near to her face.

"It's so tiny." She exclaims.
"It's so small." I'm amazed!

Pulling up her brown hair,
she hangs it on her neck.
She wonders about the meaning
of this beautiful speck.

The gift came with instructions!
Let's find out. Let's read.
Let's learn the meaning of this necklace
that has a mustard seed.

"This tiny mustard seed, no matter how small,
is extremely powerful inside this crystal ball.
When planted in cool soil...
where all the insects crawl...
it will grow up to be
the biggest tree of them all!"

It is enough to create a miracle...
All we have to do is BELIEVE!
Quite like our faith,
and we shall receive.

Suzy Lu's mother explains to Suzy Lu:

My Love, "God will answer our prayers.
All you have to do is stay true.
You shall reap what you sow,
especially someone as precious as you."

Now Suzy Lu has a big dream.
She wants seven mustard seeds,
to plant them in her garden.

She has put her little faith in action.
She prayed.
She believes she will receive!

After a while, her prayers were answered.
Suzy Lu listened and followed tradition!

For the seven mustard seeds she asked God, had finally come to fruition!

Planted in her garden,
every day...
watching from her window.
Several mustard trees grew.
Just like a crescendo.

With a big bucket,
Suzy Lu was ready to reap them all.
A full bucket and full pockets,
laughing as the seeds fall.

She BELIEVED it was TRUE,
and watched the seven mustard trees grow.
That is all she had to do
and many mustard seeds she sowed.
"A little faith is enough for God to create a miracle."
said Suzy Lu. "All we have to do is believe that
we will receive and that is what God will do."

Like this TINY MUSTARD SEED...
which in due time...became a BIG tree on a whim.

The End

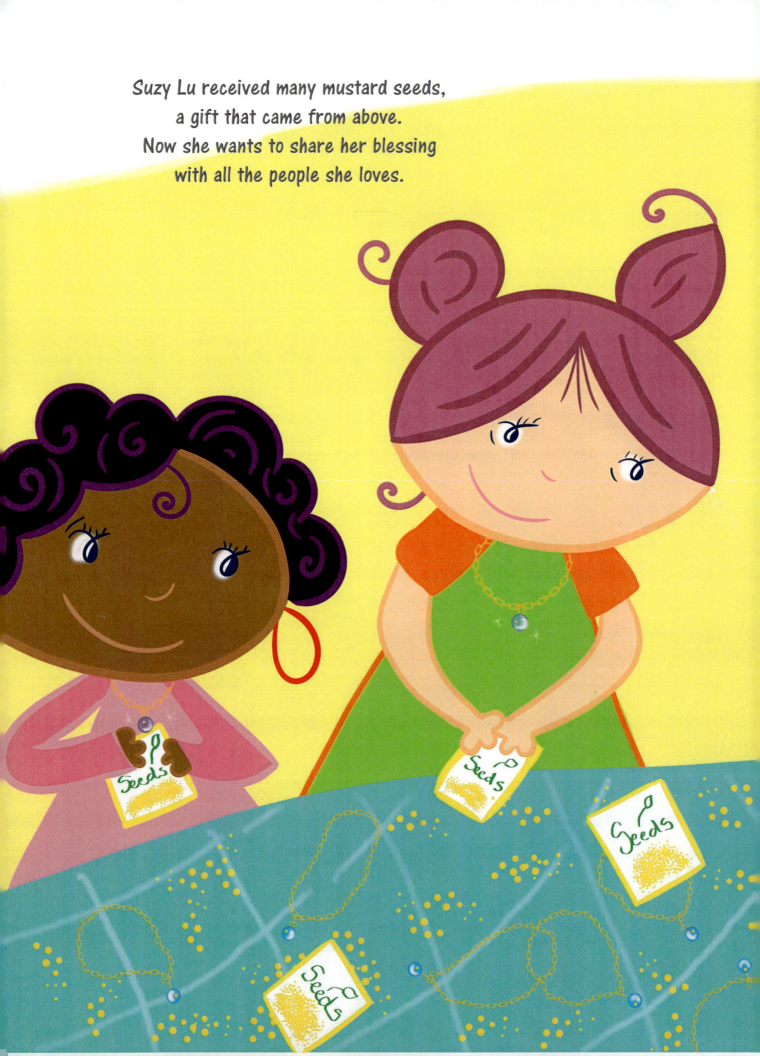

Suzy Lu received many mustard seeds,
a gift that came from above.
Now she wants to share her blessing
with all the people she loves.

Made in the USA
San Bernardino, CA
25 June 2019